C000183330

THEY DIED TOO YOUNG

RUDOLPH VALENTINO

BY
Amy Dempsey

This edition first published by Parragon Books Ltd in 1995

Produced by
Magpie Books Ltd, London

Copyright © Parragon Book Service Ltd 1995
Unit 13–17, Avonbridge Trading Estate, Atlantic Road
Avonmouth, Bristol, BS11 9QD

Illustrations courtesy of: Associated Press: Mary Evans
Picture Library; Rex Features: Aquarius Picture Library

ISBN 0 75250 836 9
A copy of the British Library Cataloguing in Publication
Data is available from the British Library.

Typeset by Hewer Text Composition Services, Edinburgh
Printed in Singapore by Printlink International Co.

THEY DIED TOO YOUNG
Rudolph Valentino

Rudolph Valentino

Rudolph Valentino was the silver screen's first and most enduring male sex-symbol – the legendary tall, dark and handsome Latin lover. His rags-to-riches tale from Italian immigrant to low-class gigolo to world-class lover was more tortured, romantic and scandalous than any that Hollywood could hope to manufacture, and one which they rewrote for the public.

Who was this man for whom millions of women grieved on his premature death, and whose very name was to become synonymous with the word 'lover'?

The Young Dreamer

On 6 May 1895 Rodolpho Alfonzo Raffaelo Pierre Filiberto Guglielmi di Valentina d'Antonguolla was born to Giovanni and Donna Beatrice Guglielmi in Castellaneta, Italy, the second of three children. The setting for Rodolpho's childhood was not remotely glamorous, but a small, backward village in southern Italy where no one ever leaves and nothing ever changes.

The family was fairly well off by peasant standards, as Giovanni was the village vet, an important position in a farming community. Little is known about Donna Beatrice, except that she was a beautiful, happy woman who loved to dance. According to local lore, it is the fact that she was always laughing and dancing while pregnant with Rodolpho that made him into such a romantic dreamer and adventurer.

The young Rodolpho spent most of his time dreaming of adventure and very little time at his studies. His main ambition was to get out of Castellaneta, and the first step came after the death of his father when Rodolpho was eleven. His mother found him difficult to manage and he was sent to school to study land surveying in Taranto, the nearest town, with his older brother, Alberto. The novelty of Taranto soon wore off and he set his sights higher, first for Rome and then finally nothing would be good enough but America, the land of opportunity. No amount of punishment could make Rodolpho concentrate on his studies and he was eventually kicked out of school. After relentless pressure from Rodolpho, and with the support of his uncle, who came to fear that he would only bring shame on the family name as a result of his womanizing and refusal to work or study, Donna Beatrice finally agreed to give Rodolpho the money his father had set aside for his education. On 9 December 1913, Rodolpho Guglielmi set sail on the SS Cleveland with a boatload of other hopeful emigrants determined to make their fortune in the United States.

Rodolpho arrived in New York two days before Christmas with little to prepare him for the move except for the address of an Italian family with relatives in Castellaneta. He made his way to West 49th Street, in the Italian quarter, where the family welcomed him into their already overcrowded apartment. For the first time, Rodolpho had a goal and realized the necessity of work. Without cash, and without his mother to bail him out, Rodolpho would not be able to take advantage of the wonders, and women, of New York. Rodolpho applied himself to learning English and worked at a number of menial jobs, from messenger to garbage collector to dishwasher. After six months his English was good enough to move away from the Italian quarter, and he got a job as an under-gardener at the Long Island home of the millionaire Cornelius Bliss. He received $6 a week plus room and board, a considerable

improvement on his earlier jobs. For
Rodolpho, however, the greatest ben-
efit was being able to observe firsthand
the type of lifestyle to which he
aspired. He studied the manners and
tastes of the rich – unfortunately, to
the neglect of his work, which led to
him being fired.

A stint working in Central Park followed, which again allowed him to
continue with his studies of the
wealthy at play. After only a few
weeks, his temper and arrogance got
him fired, and a string of occasional
part-time jobs followed. By this time,
Rodolpho was homeless and sleeping
rough in Central Park. At this low

point, in August 1914, Rodolpho was on the verge of throwing it all in and plunging himself into the East River. But he thought better of it, and decided to face the challenge that America presented.

Shortly after changing his attitude, Rodolpho got a job as a busboy in an Italian restaurant, where his fellow workers introduced him to New York's world of dancehalls and cabarets. These establishments were frequented by single and married women to meet current and future lovers, and on their terms. The women chose the men and what they wanted from them – be it to dance, sit, talk, or make love. An older waiter at the restaurant took Rodolpho under his wing and taught him to dance, and he was soon proficient enough to work as a full-time dance-partner. The tango, the new South American dance sweeping the nation, the dance of love, was Rodolpho's speciality, and he soon made the dance his own.

Rodolpho, with his Latin good looks, graceful physique and hypnotic eyes, was an instant success. He was soon earning $6 a day – what he used to earn in a week, and would happily extend his services in his dressing-room for the price of a tip or a gift. These 'love breaks', as he called them, took place between the afternoon-tea dance and the evening festivities. This job as a low-class gigolo suited Rodolpho perfectly, as he was able both to sample the wonders of the New York woman and to study her breeding and beauty at close quarters. This training would become instrumental to his later success, as he learned how to talk to women, what their fantasies were, how they wanted to be treated, how to make them feel special – in essence, how to set their passions afire. After sessions in front of the mirror, he perfected his enigmatic smile and his bedroom-eyes and could readily test their effect. He became an accomplished dancer and dresser and was

Rudolph Valentino

The young immigrant arrived in New York
full of ambition

soon hired at Maxim's, a high-class establishment, as their resident tango-dancer, not as a gigolo. He became di Valentina at this point, as it was more romantic-sounding and easier for his lovers to pronounce – they couldn't quite get their tongues around Guglielmi. Di Valentina quickly became the most popular dancer at Maxim's and began to be showered with gifts and invitations from his wealthy admirers. He was earning $70 a week and was so popular that he was no longer open to prostitution, but would accept tips from admirers if he bestowed upon them the pleasure of dancing with him. Rodolpho was well on his way to becoming a prima donna.

It was in Maxim's that Rodolpho met Bianca de Saulles, the beautiful Chilean heiress, and wife of Jack de Saulles, a prominent and wealthy New Yorker. Rodolpho asked her to dance and they danced the tango as if it was made for them alone. Rodolpho and Bianca embarked on a year-long passionate affair that was to end in scandal, the first of many to plague Rodolpho's life.

As Rodolpho's love for Bianca was so intense, he decided to become a legitimate professional dancer, first teaming up with Bonnie Glass, with whom he performed for President Wilson, and then with Joan Sawyer. Meanwhile,

Bianca and Rodolpho were plotting a way to catch her husband, Jack, in an adulterous act, the only grounds for divorce in New York. The social-climbing Joan Sawyer was to provide the perfect bait for the womanizing Jack. Rodolpho and Bianca introduced the pair and arranged for them to be caught in the act. The divorce was granted in Bianca's favour, with Rodolpho named as one of the witnesses. De Saulles was not happy and set Rodolpho up to be charged with blackmail. Although the charges were dropped, Rodolpho was in over his head and fearful of being deported. He thought it best to get out of town until things died down. He went on a dance tour to wait until he and Bianca could be together. In his absence, in August 1917, Bianca shot and killed Jack over custody of their child, and Rodolpho, fearful of his involvement being brought up again, did what many a man would do in such a situation – headed West.

His first stop was San Francisco, where he was horrified to discover that no one had heard of him. He landed a part in the chorus line of a show that was short-lived, but made contacts that were not. The most important of these was with Norman Kerry, a young actor just beginning to make it in Hollywood. He befriended

Rodolpho and offered to show him the ropes, and was to prove a valuable and genuine friend over the years.

Hollywood

Next stop – Hollywood. Norman
Kerry put Rodolpho up while he
made the rounds, queuing for bit
parts for $5 a day. His foreign looks
went against him at this time in Hollywood as the taste of the day was the
clean-cut American apple pie image.
The only roles open to him were small
parts as thieves or gangsters. He soon
became discouraged and returned to

the professions in which he knew he could make a living – dancing and prostitution. Rodolpho's first break came through Norman Kerry, whose friend, the director Emmett Flynn, gave Rodolpho a bit part as a dancer in *Alimony*. It was but a few seconds on screen, but di Valentina was hooked and set his sights higher.

Soon after, the star Mae Murray, and her husband, the director Bob Leonard, spotted Rodolpho dancing at the Vernon Club. Mae, wanting to do more than dance with the handsome Italian, insisted he play the leading man in her new film, *The Big Little Person*. She put her all into the love scenes, and demanded him for her next film, *The Delicious Little Devil*. Rodolpho couldn't believe his luck – he was earning $100 a week and his name was second only to Mae Murray's! The love scenes were even hotter and heavier than in the first picture, and although Bob Leonard maintained his professional poise, there was not to be a third picture with his wife. It was, however, the start that Rodolpho needed, and Bob Leonard even re-commended him for his next film.

Rodolpho felt he was on the brink of success and that he needed an image, so he went about creating one. The image he decided to cultivate was that

Jean Acker, Valentino's first wife

As Julio in *The Four Horsemen of the Apocalypse*

of the mysterious loner – someone who was special, different, an enigma. He bought two white Russian wolfhounds and a white bathing-suit, which showed off his body and tan nicely, and strolled along the beaches of Santa Monica, alone except for his dogs. Rodolpho had realized at an early stage in his career the verity of that famous maxim: it doesn't matter what people are saying – as long as they are talking about you. And talk they did.

Rodolpho's next picture, *A Society Sensation*, was with Carmel Meyers, a fifteen-year-old starlet. The two became good friends but nothing more,

as Carmel's mother forbade any relationship developing, because of her
age. He made another film with
Meyers, *All Night*, and was given a
pay rise, which he promptly used for
the down payment on a huge Merce.
This complemented his developing
image nicely, as he knew he cut a
fine figure in his fast car with an
ever-changing line-up of beautiful
companions.

After this, Rodolpho's luck took a turn
for the worse, and he was reduced to
dancing in the prologue to warm up
the audience for a D.W. Griffith film
for which he had unsuccessfully audi-
tioned, *Scarlet Days*. His car and the

loner image had to be returned for the time being, and Rodolpho became despondent. At about the same time, he received news that his mother had died. In the midst of his despair, he became even more determined to prove himself for her. Rodolpho's fortune was, however, to get worse before it could get better.

In order to cheer himself up and hopefully make some new contacts, Rodolpho accepted an invitation to a small dinner party at the Ship's Café in honour of the Russian film star, Alla Nazimova. As Rodolpho was being introduced, Nazimova froze him out and thundered to his companion,

'How dare you bring that gigolo to my table!' she proceeded to recount the de Saulles scandal from New York. Rodolpho left in shame and the table was shocked into silence – not at the gossip, as Rodolpho would have thought, but at the appalling behavior of Nazimova. The party soon disbanded. Rodolpho was horrified that the story would go around Hollywood. It did. But to his surprise people were angry on his behalf.

The aspiring starlet, Jean Acker, one of Nazimova's lesbian circle, was one who went out of her way to express her sympathy for Rodolpho. Rodolpho, vulnerable after the death of his

23

mother and Nazimova's humiliation, was particularly susceptible to a sympathetic companion. He was completely taken with Acker and thought he had found his soul mate. Whether unaware of her sexual orientation or arrogant enough to think he could change it, Rodolpho was determined to conquer her. A few days after they met, he took her horse-riding by moonlight to convince her of his devotion. Caught up in the romance of the situation, Acker agreed to his marriage proposal and they were married by special licence the next day. After the wedding party, things went downhill quickly. Rodolpho, eager to consummate the marriage, was

bewildered and hurt when Acker,
faced with the reality of her actions
– heterosexual sex – shut him out of
her Hollywood Hotel apartment. It
was the ultimate humiliation, a mock-
ery of his machismo, his sexuality: the
man who would become known as the
world's greatest lover was spurned by
his wife on his wedding night, and not
even for another man. To make matters worse, the humiliation was again
public, as a group of the couple's
friends were waiting outside the apartment window to cheer them on. The
only good thing to come of the
marriage was Acker's suggestion that
he change his name to 'Rudolph
Valentino'.

Smouldering passion in *The Sheik*

Gloria Swanson, Valentino's co-star in
Beyond the Rocks

This year, 1919, was to be one of mixed blessings. While full of heartbreak, it was also the same year as Valentino's big break in the film industry. June Mathis, the top screenwriter of the day, head-hunted Valentino to play Julio, the Latin hero in *The Four Horsemen of the Apocalypse* by Vicente Blasco Ibanez. It was a highly coveted role and Valentino couldn't believe his luck. He was given $350 a week, a star's dressing-room, a suite at the Hollywood Hotel, and detailed coaching from Mathis and the director, Rex Ingram, whose heads were on the line if hiring Valentino, a relative unknown, didn't prove worth the gamble.

The main advice from Mathis was for Valentino to rely on his eyes to get across most of the character's inner feeling and emotions; to play the part with restraint. All those sessions in New York practising speaking and seducing with his eyes were to pay off. The intensity, perseverance and dedication of Mathis, Ingram and Valentino paid off, as the early rushes proved. A tango scene was included which was so breathtaking that no one could suggest any improvements. Metro was convinced it was backing a winner, and the star-making machinery was set in motion. A glamorous background was created for Valentino, in which he had attended the Royal

Military Academy, was a world travel-
ler, and had received his facial scar in a
duel in Paris, protecting a lady's honour. With eight months to wait before
the picture premièred, Valentino made
another film with Metro, *Uncharted
Seas*, and was able to resuscitate his
image as the mysterious loner with a
flashy sports car. Because of the Acker
problems, he kept his romantic activ-
ities out of the limelight.

While filming *Uncharted Seas*, Alla
Nazimova came to the set one day
to watch him rehearse. Ever-unpre-
dictable, she now wanted the 'gigolo'
to play opposite her in *Camille*, which
was to resuscitate her career. She

introduced Valentino to Natacha
Rambova, her latest protégée, a costume and set designer. 'I saw before
me no ordinary woman, but rather the
reincarnation of some mighty goddess
of the past.' Valentino was captivated
and immediately under her spell. Natacha, born Winifred Shaughnessy in
Salt Lake City, Utah, the stepdaughter
of the US cosmetics millionaire, Ri-
chard Hudnut, was dynamic, domi-
neering, and beautiful. She went to
school in England, trained with the
Imperial Russian Ballet, and, since
meeting Nazimova, had adopted a
new and impressive name and
decided to begin a career in the film
world. She was rich and cosmopolitan,

but also strong-willed, manipulative, and incredibly ambitious. Natacha originally found Valentino irritating, beneath her, tiresome. But, realizing that Nazimova's reign of power in Hollywood was coming to an end and Valentino's was just beginning, she quickly switched camps. During the filming of *Camille* Natacha successfully played both sides of the fence. She would accompany Nazimova on her rounds of choosing evening companions – feeling the bodies of a line-up of topless girls. She also held up the film's shooting and kept Nazimova waiting on a number of occasions by afternoons of intense and passionate sex with Valentino in his dressing-room. She had Valentino under her control and she used this power to manipulate and dominate him. Rudolph became Natacha's 'project', her art form. Her career was Valentino — to make him a 'great artiste'. Thanks to her, he would lose work, friends, directors, studios — she was to be his greatest love and his worst nightmare.

Meanwhile, in January 1921, in the midst of his success and new love, a black cloud appeared in the form of Jean Acker. Out of work, Acker filed for maintenance, claiming that Valentino had refused to live with her and had deserted her. Valentino hired a top

lawyer and fortunately had saved letters to and from Acker. He filed for
divorce. This was to be the first of
many expensive, sensational court
cases in Valentino's life.

The Great Lover

In March of 1921, *The Four Horsemen of the Apocalypse* opened simultaneously in New York, Chicago, and Boston. It fulfilled all box-office expectations: it was hailed as a masterpiece, Valentino as a star, and it eventually headed Variety's list of top grossers for the 1920s. Valentino danced and smouldered his way into the hearts of women all over the country.

After his success, he asked for a rise. Metro only offered $50 a week more, so, on Natacha's insistence, he quit. The gamble paid off this time. After eight months of doing nothing, Jesse Lasky of Paramount called Valentino to play the lead in a film of the new best seller *The Sheik* by E.M. Hull. E.M. Hull was actually Edith Maud Winstanley, a Derbyshire pig-farmer's wife who wrote racy romantic novels to help make ends meet. The story finds the beautiful and fair heroine, Diana Mayo, captured in the Arabian desert by a brutal, albeit handsome, beast of a sheik who forces her into sexual acts against her will and awakens in her a passion that she didn't know existed, a passion that must be resisted. The struggles as the sheik forces her into submission, half-desirous, half-resisting, hit a nerve with women worldwide. It was the erotic made permissible by the exotic; written not by a world-travelling man, but by a woman who knew what women of her day wanted. This included the all-important happy ending, and E.M. Hull knew how to reassure her public: the sheik is revealed to be an English peer who was brought up in the desert − of course, through no fault of his own − and Diana declares undying love for him.

The Great Lover

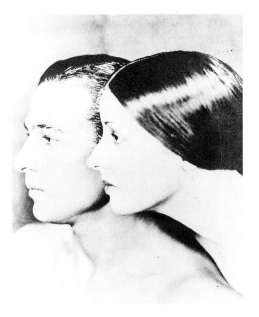

Valentino and Natacha Rambova

While the critics, and Natacha, scorned the book as trash, the public decided otherwise. Although Natacha vehemently disapproved of Valentino taking the role, he did, starting at $500 a week. The reviews of the film wrote it off as an unrealistic desert romance – exactly that which made the female public flock to see it in droves. As far as the female audience was concerned, it had it all: romance, excitement, passion, adventure, exotic foreigners, domination, brutality, true love. The reception would be quite different today, of course, but it is not hard to believe that the hearts and hormones of women all over the world were set afire by the film. Valentino's reputation as the Great Lover was made.

The film broke all previous box-office records, amassing $2,000,000 in two years and over 125,000,000 people went to see it. It influenced fashion and language: harem-pants became the rage and the word 'sheik' came to mean a masterful husband or lover, even as a dictionary entry! The film and its fans made Rudolph Valentino the screen's first male sex-symbol. The resulting hysteria found Valentino mobbed wherever he went and receiving over 1,000 fan letters a week. The letters contained nude photographs, rude propositions, and items of underwear from women desperate to gain the Love God's attention and affection.

The divorce hearing between Acker and Valentino came about in the midst of all this mania, in November 1921, sending Hollywood gossips and journalists into a media frenzy. Acker sued for maintenance and Valentino filed for divorce, stating that the marriage had never been consummated. Valentino professed his love for Acker and said that he had thought she was a 'normal' woman when they married. Acker finally admitted that they had never slept together, and she left the court in the arms of a female friend as the divorce was granted in Valentino's favor, due to Acker's desertion. Valentino agreed to pay Acker $12,100 to prevent further claims against him, and borrowed the money from Paramount. During the celebrations at a local speakeasy that night, Valentino was elated when Natacha accepted his proposal of marriage, unaware that he was about to enter an even more destructive union.

For fans and detractors of Valentino alike, the developments of the trial were too good to be true – increasing women's desire to help and love the Great Lover, and providing fodder for rumours about his masculinity for his

With Nita Valdi in *Blood and Sand*

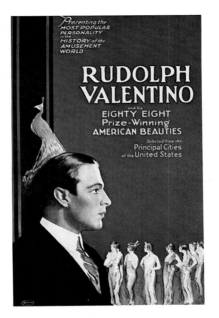

The Great Lover goes on tour

critics, mostly men threatened by the effect he had on their women.

Valentino made two more films with Paramount right after *The Sheik*, *Moran of the Lady Letty* and *Beyond the Rocks* with Gloria Swanson. There was no love lost between Valentino and Swanson, and Natacha did not help matters. He was now earning $1,000 a week and making everyone involved in the films' production miserable by the on-set presence of Natacha. Under her control he became hypercritical, uncooperative, demanding, and complained constantly about his need for artistic recognition. It was only through the intervention of Jesse

Lasky that both films were completed without major disruptions or staff walk-outs. Valentino's 'artistic needs' were temporarily appeased when he was next offered the role of Juan Gallardo in another Ibanez costume-drama, *Blood and Sand*. Valentino was ecstatic, as it was his favourite type of role, with elaborate costumes and semi-nude scenes to show off his body, and bullfighting scenes to display his manliness. Valentino insisted on learning to bullfight and doing the scenes himself. Again, Lasky had to intervene to bring the egos of Valentino, Natacha, and the director, Fred Niblo, into a cease-fire in order to complete the picture. An early rough cut showed Valentino to have delivered a brilliant performance, and Paramount hired more people to be on the publicity and legend-making team.

Riding high, Natacha and Rudolph went across the border and were married on 13 May 1922 in the small town of Mexicali, Mexico. After celebrating with the mayor and his wife, who threw them a surprise party, the couple headed to Palm Springs to begin their honeymoon. The news that greeted them was to send them spinning. They had not waited the legally required year after his divorce from Acker, and, as such, the marriage in Mexico was a bigamous one. While this law was broken regularly by couples, Rudolph's timing was bad. The Hays Commission had just been set up in Los Angeles to clean up the films and lives of those in the film industry. Valentino was arrested and thrown in jail for bigamy as an example of the seriousness with which the District Attorney's office was taking its new job.

To Valentino's horror, his lawyers and the studio advised him to testify that he and Natacha had not slept together since the wedding – in effect, to publicly announce that he, the Great Lover, had not consummated *either* of his marriages. As the other alternative

was the very real possibility of a one-
to five-year jail sentence, which most
certainly would have been enforced
due to the high-profile nature of the
case, Valentino obeyed the lawyers
and sheepishly testified that, due to
illness and the presence of friends, he
and Natacha had not yet slept together. The charges were dropped.

Paramount claimed that the trial was
worth $1 million in free publicity but
the cost to Valentino was sacrificing his
pride and manliness in yet another
sensational public humiliation. Rudolph did himself no favours by insisting on *The Young Rajah* for his next film,
in which he appeared in a costume

consisting of a jewelled jockstrap and strings of pearls draped around his body. Although Natacha had been sent to her parents' home in the Adirondacks, New York, during the trial and film her influence was ever-present in the form of daily correspondence and critiques and in the form of unfortunate 'artistic' decisions – Valentino's choice of film and costume. At her prompting, he announced he would not attend the premières of the film, as an 'artiste' should not be subjected to mauling by hysterical fans. On a roll, he also demanded the right of script approval for all his future films as a condition of staying with Paramount.

Poster for the film *Monsieur Beaucaire*

Valentino and Natacha say farewell

The morning after completing the film, Rudolph went east to join Natacha, who 'helped' him prepare a statement saying he was leaving Paramount due to artistic differences. Paramount filed an injunction preventing him from working with other studios. Valentino rejected an offer of $7,000 a week and the right to consultation over films and directors, and the case went to court. The case was decided in Paramount's favour, such that Valentino either had to honour his contract with them or retire from the film business until February 1924.

While these legal wrangles were going on, Natacha and Rudolph became

involved in spiritualism. Valentino
seemed to have an uncanny natural
psychic ability and was able to contact
his spirit guide, Black Feather, an
American Indian, without a medium.
Rudolph now had two sources of
guidance in the forms of Natacha
and Black Feather. While the gamble
with Paramount did not go in his
favour, he remained optimistic as
Black Feather predicted a tour of
America for the couple which would
reap financial rewards and new friends.

One of many people following the
case with interest was the entrepre-
neur, S. George Ullmann. Knowing of
the couple's financial difficulties, he

made them an offer even Natacha couldn't refuse: $7,000 a week (equal to Paramount's offer) to do a dance tour of the country to endorse the cosmetics by Mineralava Beauty Clay Company. Valentino liked Ullmann and his business sense, and even Natacha agreed more readily than expected – she too was aware of their finances, and since Black Feather had predicted such a project, it did not seem too beneath her.

The couple finally married on 14 March 1923 in Crown Point, Indiana, witnessed by Natacha's aunt, Theresa Werner, and George Ullmann. The company travelled in a lavish private railroad car Ullmann hired for the tour, complete with gilt mirrors, Turkish carpets, chef and dining room. The tour began in Omaha, Nebraska, in a blizzard, where fans made their way through the adverse conditions to a sold-out show. This success was repeated at every stop on the tour, with fans lining the track for the couple's arrival and departure, and making record attendances at the theaters where they danced. The show opened with the couple dancing the tango, followed by a few words about the company's products, and a beauty contest judged by Valentino. It then closed with Valentino and Natacha re-enacting the scene from *The Four Horsemen of the Apocalypse* for which he was famous.

These live performances kept Valentino in front of his fans during his enforced retirement from the screen and, capitalizing on this wave of attention, his old films were re-released. The devotion of Valentino's fans increased daily and it reached fever pitch with the publication of *Daydreams*, a collection of love poems written by Valentino during the year he and Natacha were forbidden to wed. The press covered every movement of the glamorous and romantic couple.

Ullmann, now Valentino's personal manager, set about trying to sort out his financial mess. He cleared many of Valentino's debts and negotiated a deal with Paramount which required him to make two more films for them and then they would release him to join the new movie company, Ritz-Carlton Pictures. When the announcement was made that Valentino would be returning to the silver screen, thousands of women mobbed the hotel where Valentino was staying in New York.

In London for the première of *The Eagle*

With Vilma Banky in *Son of the Sheik*

The Misguided Hero

With matters seemingly in order, Valentino and Natacha were now free to go to Europe on a belated honeymoon which was to culminate in a visit to his home town. The trip started off well, with enthusiastic receptions and spending frenzies in London and Paris, and a visit to Natacha's parents in Nice. From Nice they drove to Italy to meet Valentino's brother and sister. A combination of bad temper on Natacha's part and bad driving on Rudolph's pushed Natacha to her limit, and by the time they reached Rome she turned back for Nice and her mother. The rest of the pilgrimage to Castellaneta was made by Rudolph, sister Maria, brother Alberto, and Natacha's aunt, Theresa. Alberto advised against the trip, saying that it would be a disappointment, but Rudolph was determined. They drove into town, visited the few neighbours who remembered him from his childhood (but who had never seen a film, much less one of his) visited the cemetery and the old house and drove out. Nothing had changed.

Back in Hollywood, the last two films made for Paramount were a disaster on all fronts. Natacha's interference was even worse than before, as she seemed both jealous of her husband's success and the attention that accompanied it and insistent on it. The films (*Monsieur Beaucaire* and *A Sainted Devil*) were critical failures and Paramount was overjoyed to hand its 'number one nightmare' over to Ritz-Carlton.

The contract with Ritz-Carlton gave the couple complete artistic control and they used it to destroy themselves and the company. The first film they chose was written by Natacha, *The Hooded Falcon*, set in medieval Spain.

Natacha would also direct the film and insist on a trip to Spain to acquire authentic costumes and props. During the 'looting of Spain' the couple spent $100,000 of the studio's money on antiques alone, and the escalating pre-production costs of the film sent Ritz-Carlton into liquidation.

For Christmas that year, Natacha designed, and had made by Tiffany's, a platinum slave bracelet for her husband. Valentino loved it and vowed never to remove it. Despite jeers in the press, he never did. Valentino was constantly plagued by speculation about his sexual orientation and masculinity, and the bracelet did not help

True to form, Valentino made a grand exit

RUDOLPH VALENTINO
IN "THE SON OF THE SHEIK"

Memories of Rudolph Valentino

matters. The American male could not understand, and was threatened by, the effect this camp Continental had on American women. The bracelet was a potent symbol of Natacha's power over Valentino and of the dependence that was destroying his career.

With the collapse of Ritz–Carlton, the couple had an emergency meeting with Ullmann, who had an offer for Valentino from United Artists. They were offering $1 million a year, but with a strict stipulation that Natacha have no part at all. While Natacha protested and hurled abuse, Valentino finally reached his limit and stood up to her for the first time: 'You have cost me my friends and humiliated me in public; you have mocked my work and abused my talent. But this time I will do things my way.' He signed the contract, and effectively the death certificate for his marriage.

Natacha was devastated by his disloyalty, and played on his guilt to have him finance her first film, *What Price Beauty?* The film was far from a success and this further exacerbated their domestic problems. Without control over Valentino's career, which she had made her own, Natacha rapidly lost interest in Valentino the man. She announced that she was moving to New York, supposedly to look for a distributor for her film. She left on 13 August, 1924 and hundreds of fans gathered for what would turn out to be their final kiss. Upon arriving in New York, Natacha discussed with the press their need for a 'marital vacation' – to Rudolph's consternation. He was originally despondent and suicidal at their separation, but then began to reacquaint himself with old friends whom Natacha had alienated. He began to enjoy himself, making the rounds on the party circuit, an activity that Natacha despised and forbade when they were together.

Valentino's first film for United Artists was *The Eagle*. At its première in New York in November 1925, Valentino was mobbed and the crowd stamped its feet for more. He needed a five-man team of bodyguards to walk from his hotel to the limousine; the reception was even more overwhelming and hysterical than before. Valentino was still the undisputed champion of the box office and, perhaps more importantly, it proved to Valentino that it was he who held the power to his success.

On 10 November, 1925 Rudolph Valentino applied for US citizenship, the same day that Natacha returned from Europe and two days after she had applied for divorce in Paris. The two did not meet. On the 14th,

Rudolph set sail for England for the
European première of *The Eagle*. The
film was received equally well in
Europe and Valentino was hailed as a
hero. In January 1926 the divorce
between Natacha and Rudolph Valentino was granted with neither party
in attendance. Valentino returned to
New York a free man, and the most
eligible bachelor in America.

For the first time since he became a
sex symbol, Rudolph Valentino was a
single man. His fans were in hysterical
overdrive, and his Hollywood collea-
gues were not much better. Pola
Negri, the Polish actress, was one
who made a public play for his

affections: 'Once Rudy has experienced my love, he will forget about all other women. I am ready when he is.' She stalked Valentino and they were eventually set up by Marion Davis. Negri became his almost constant companion, and helped to exorcize the memory of Natacha and to lay to rest the rumours that marriages to two dominant women had depleted his manhood. Alberto, Rudolph's brother, who was now living in Hollywood, did not approve of this public, immoral relationship, but Rudolph countered that he was just living up to his reputation as the Great Lover.

This reputation was to be further enhanced by his next film, *The Son of the Sheik*, from E.M. Hull's latest novel. The main aim of the film was to exploit the ever-growing legend of Valentino the Love God, and it was an incredible hit. Upon completion of the film, Valentino suffered from post-production depression which manifested itself in fast, reckless driving. He smashed his beloved Isotta Fraschini. The studio executives were in a panic about the safety of their star and forbade him to drive alone or in excess of 50 m.p.h.

As if he had a view to the future, perhaps from Black Feather, Valentino began to make amends to those relationships destroyed by his with Natacha. One such friend was June Mathis, whom Natacha had given a hard time while working on *The Hooded Falcon*. They spoke about old times and Valentino's early days, and his spirits began to lift.

A week later, he set off east to publicize *The Son of the Sheik*, seen off by Pola Negri — the last time she would see him alive. The success of *The Son of the Sheik* was rather qualified for Rudolph, as attacks on his 'powder puff' effeminacy were started by the press in Chicago. Pink powder-puff dispensers had been installed in men's restrooms and Valentino was being held responsible for the feminization of the American male. Instead of letting it lie and blow over, as Ullmann advised, Rudolph was determined to defend his manhood and started an exchange of letters in the press from New York, challenging the journalist to a boxing match. While the match did not take place, Rudolph felt vindicated, although his reputation would have fared better had he gracefully ignored the jibe.

Back in New York after the success of the Chicago première, Rudolph began a round of wild partying. He also continued to put his affairs in order.

He was reconciled with Jean Acker and even apologized to Adolph Zukor of Paramount for all the trouble he had caused the studio. The summer was filled with a whirlwind of personal appearances and parties, and the pace began to take its toll. Rudolph had been suffering from stomach pains for some time, but, with his peasant's fear of doctors, had refused to have it checked, insisting that it was just indigestion. The rounds of partying continued.

On 14 August 1926 Valentino, against the wishes of Ullmann, who thought he was looking a bit worn out, went to another all-night party held in his honor. The next morning Ullmann found him writing on the floor of his hotel room, clutching his stomach. He was immediately rushed to New York's Polyclinic Hospital and operated on that evening for acute appendicitis and an undiagnosed gastric ulcer. The operation initially seemed a success, and extra staff had to be hired at the hospital to cope with the calls and gifts from well-wishers from all over America and the world.

A few days later, Rudolph was feeling much better and announced that he would be able to leave the hospital within a few days. The doctors took this rapid cessation of pain to be a bad

sign and did another examination.
Complications had set in, including
poisoning of the wall of the heart.
On Monday morning he awoke in
great pain and was given a morphine
injection. Rudolph was still optimistic
that he would have a speedy recovery
but later that day became delirious
with fever, rambling irrationally in
Italian and English. By the next morning he had slipped into a coma and two
priests, one from his home town,
administered the last rites of the Ro-
man Catholic Church. Shortly before
noon on 23 August 1926, 'with a
priest's crucifix pressed to his lips',
Rudolph Valentino died 'without
pain' at the age of thirty-one.

The World Grieves

The news of his premature death was received with shock and incomprehension. Young girls took to wearing black armbands. Flags were lowered to half-mast. One fan who could not cope with the news was Peggy Scott, a young actress living in London, who committed suicide, leaving a note asking for someone to care for her shrine of photographs of Valentino.

Charlie Chaplin said: 'The death of Rudolph Valentino is one of the greatest tragedies that has occurred in the history of the motion picture industry. As an actor, he attained fame and distinction; as a friend, he commanded love and admiration. We of the film industry, through his death, lose a very dear friend, a man of great charm and kindliness.'

Rudolph Valentino's last public appearance was even more hysterical than those when he was alive. His body was laid to rest in a bronze coffin at Frank E. Campbell's Broadway funeral home, and over 12,000 people gathered outside the chapel. The pressure of the crowd, as they moved towards the building, shattered the chapel window, raining glass on the mourners, and a riot broke out between the police and the fans. Once order was restored, the doors were opened, and the crowd filed through rows of policemen to pay their last respects. Over 40,000 people had viewed the body by the time the doors closed on the first day and 50,000 made the trip the following day. By this time, the whole thing had become such a fiasco that George Ullmann reversed his decision and only allowed family and friends for the next few days before the funeral.

Streets were closed and an escort of twelve policemen on motorcycles was required to move the coffin from the funeral home to the church of St. Malachy for the funeral. Spectators lined the route, causing a riot as they gathered for a last glimpse of their idol. Celebrities turned out in full force – Jean Acker, Pola Negri, Mary Pickford, Douglas Fairbanks and Gloria Swanson were but a few to attend the invitation-only funeral service. A nurse and doctor were on call to deal with emotional emergencies, and there was fainting on the part of Jean Acker. Valentino's exit was in grand style, befitting the apotheosis of the Love God.

The body was then sent by train to California for its last journey. Fears that the body would be taken to Italy were alleviated by Alberto: 'My brother belonged to America and his resting-place will be in California, which he loved. My sister feels this way, too.' Along the route, people turned out at the stations to pay their respects. On 7 September a mass was held at the Church of the Good Shepherd in Beverly Hills before the burial. He was buried in June Mathis's family crypt at the Hollywood Cemetery while blossoms were dropped from a plane overhead.

At his death, Valentino's affairs were a mess, and the job of cleaning it up fell to George Ullmann. He auctioned off books, ties, socks, etc. to an eager public for $76,000. Valentino left a third of his will to Alberto and to Maria, and to Theresa Werner, as an expression of gratitude for her kindness after the divorce. Jean Acker received nothing and Natacha Rambova received one dollar. The Great Lover had finally redressed the balance in death as he had not been able to in life.

FURTHER MINI SERIES
INCLUDE

THEY DIED TOO YOUNG

Elvis
James Dean
Buddy Holly
Jimi Hendrix
Sid Vicious
Marc Bolan
Ayrton Senna
Marilyn Monroe
Jim Morrison